WHEN THE WOLVES RETURNED

RESTORING NATURE'S BALANCE IN YELLOWSTONE

DOROTHY HINSHAW PATENT

PHOTOGRAPHS BY DAN HARTMAN AND CASSIE HARTMAN

WALKER & COMPANY
New York

To Brian Connolly, who planted the seeds from which this book grew —D. H. P. and D. H.

To all of those who enjoy the outdoors —C. H.

With thanks to Nathan Varley for his suggestions for the manuscript —D. H. P.

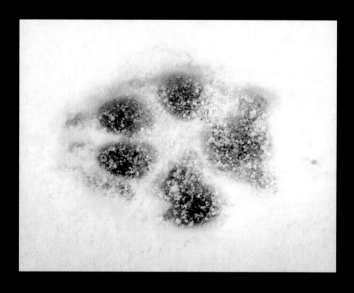

Text copyright © 2008 by Dorothy Hinshaw Patent
Photographs copyright © 2008 by Dan Hartman and Cassie Hartman

First published in the United States of America in 2008 by Walker Publishing Company, Inc.
Distributed to the trade by Macmillan

For information about permission to reproduce selections from this book, write to
Permissions, Walker & Company, 175 Fifth Avenue, New York, New York 10010

Library of Congress Cataloging-in-Publication Data
Patent, Dorothy Hinshaw.
When the wolves returned : restoring nature's balance in Yellowstone / Dorothy Hinshaw Patent ;
photographs by Dan and Cassie Hartman.
p.   cm.
ISBN-13: 978-0-8027-9686-8 • ISBN-10: 0-8027-9686-9 (hardcover)
ISBN-13: 978-0-8027-9687-5 • ISBN-10: 0-8027-9687-7 (reinforced)
1. Wolves—Reintroduction—Yellowstone National Park—Juvenile literature. 2. Wolves—Reintroduction—Yellowstone National Park—
Pictorial works. 3. Yellowstone National Park—Juvenile literature. I. Hartman, Dan, ill. II. Hartman, Cassie, ill. III. Title.
QL737.C22P385 2008   599.773'1770978752—dc22   2007037141

Typeset in Avenir

Book design by Nicole Gastonguay

Visit Walker & Company's Web site at www.walkeryoungreaders.com

Printed in China
4 6 8 10 9 7 5 3 (hardcover)
2 4 6 8 10 9 7 5 3 (reinforced)

All papers used by Walker & Company are natural, recyclable products made from wood grown in well-managed forests.
The manufacturing processes conform to the environmental regulations of the country of origin.

Yellowstone is a very special place.

IMAGINE A LAND WHERE giant geysers blow jets of steam hundreds of feet into the chilly evening air, and large herds of elk graze along the river shore. That was Yellowstone in the 1800s, a magical region tucked into the northwestern corner of Wyoming—a place where nature had been allowed to take its course with little human interference.

More than a hundred years ago, America turned Yellowstone into the world's first national park.

YELLOWSTONE CONTAINS MORE natural geologic wonders than any other place on Earth—steaming mud pots, boiling hot pools, jetting geysers, and a fabulous, colorful canyon with stunning waterfalls. The government realized what a treasure the area was, and in 1872 the United States Congress declared it to be a national park.

For many years, the most important thing was that people enjoy the park.

"FOR THE BENEFIT ENJOYMENT OF THE

THE ORIGINAL PURPOSE FOR THE PARK was to preserve its geologic wonders for visitors. The plants and animals were merely a bonus. People were even allowed to hunt the wildlife and cut down the trees. In the early days, the effects of these activities were slight, since few people made the long, hard trip to reach the park. But as transportation improved and more people came, their impact grew.

Because wolves fed on the elk and deer that people liked, hunters were paid to kill the wolves. By 1926 the wolves were all gone.

IN THE EARLY YEARS, the park officials didn't understand that predators like wolves are just as important in nature as plant eaters like elk. They thought killing predators would help the elk and other big game animals.

Safe from wolves, elk became more numerous as the years passed.

WHEN THE WEATHER WAS MILD, many elk calves survived, and the population swelled. But during severe winters, the population would crash as thousands starved. To control the elk, park rangers trapped many of them and sent them to other parks and preserves. Rangers also had to shoot and kill them by the hundreds to keep their numbers down.

Coyotes also increased in number, taking over the land and food that other small predators need to survive.

WITHOUT WOLVES at the top of the food chain, coyotes became Yellowstone's main top predator. Coyotes feed on everything from elk calves to insects but mostly on small rodents like ground squirrels. So many coyotes made it harder for other small predators, like foxes and badgers, to thrive.

The coyotes fed on newborn pronghorn, so every year, fewer pronghorn fawns survived.

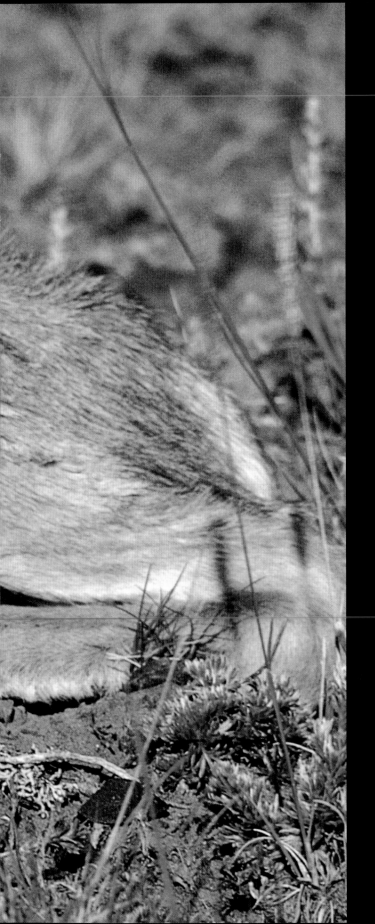

THE COYOTES IN YELLOWSTONE became experts at finding newborn pronghorn fawns. With so many coyotes in the park, pronghorn numbers dropped. Park managers worried that pronghorn might disappear completely.

Even the trees and shrubs in the park suffered because the wolves were gone.

BECAUSE SO MANY ELK were eating the young shoots and bark, few young aspen trees, cottonwood trees, and willow shrubs grew to replace the old ones that died. Before long, the songbirds that lived and nested in these trees and bushes became rare.

The beavers that need aspens, cottonwoods, and willows also began to disappear.

BEAVERS LIVE IN RIVERS AND STREAMS, where they use their strong, sharp teeth to cut down trees like aspens. They store them to eat during the winter. They also use the trees to build dams and their homes, called lodges. Beaver dams create ponds that provide homes for many different animals, from dragonflies to ducks to moose.

Unable to survive without the trees they needed, the beavers were almost gone from the northern part of the park by the 1950s.

Some scientists thought forest fires might fix Yellowstone, but they were wrong.

IN 1988 WEATHER CONDITIONS created a situation perfect for wildfire in the park. Almost a million acres burned. Scientists expected the new shoots that would grow from roots of burned willows and aspens would provide plenty of healthy new bushes and trees, but the elk ate most of them.

Scientists finally decided that returning the wolf might help solve the park's problems.

FOR THOUSANDS OF YEARS, wolves lived in Yellowstone along with the other animals. Many of the problems in the park began soon after the wolves were eliminated. After studying the problem, scientists predicted that returning wolves could control the numbers of coyotes and elk. This, scientists believed, would allow other living things, like aspens and ground squirrels, to thrive once more.

Many people fought the idea of bringing back wolves, but they lost the battle.

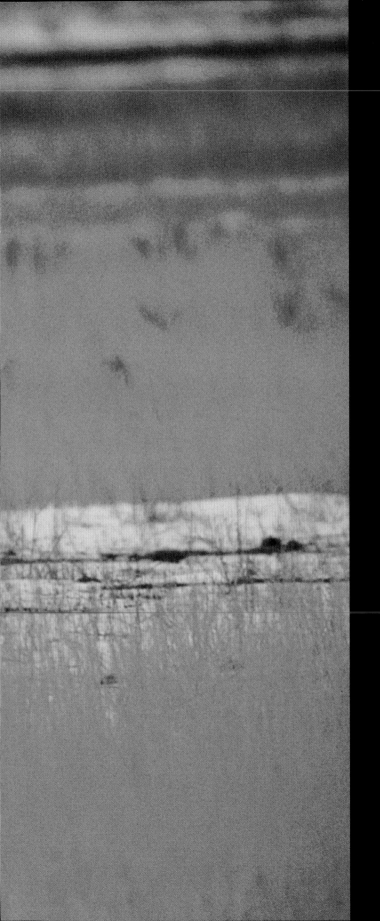

Save 100 Elk
KILL A WOLF!

RANCHERS LIVING NEARBY worried that the wolves would leave the park to prey on their cattle or sheep. But most Americans believed it was time for wolves to return.

Wolves trapped in Canada were brought to Yellowstone in 1995 and 1996. Seven groups of wolves were set free in different parts of the park. Each group, called a pack, lived in a wide area called a territory. It didn't take long for them to feel at home as there was plenty of prey—especially elk—for them to hunt.

When the wolves were brought back, they thrived and multiplied.

YEAR BY YEAR, the number of wolves in Yellowstone grew. When a pack became too big, it broke into smaller packs that slowly filled the habitat in the vast park. Now, about twelve wolf packs live in the park. The total wolf population varies, but there are usually around 150 wolves.

Wolves chased and killed the coyotes until half of them were gone.

WOLVES ARE MUCH BIGGER and stronger than coyotes, and they saw the coyotes as competition. They killed them or chased them from their territories.

Now the coyotes are learning how to survive around wolves, and their numbers are increasing again. They often feed on the remains of wolf kills, but they stay out of the wolves' way.

With fewer coyotes hunting them, pronghorn and other prey animals survive more easily.

WITH FEWER COYOTES on the prowl, more pronghorn fawns can survive, helping this graceful animal grow in numbers. The pronghorn population appears to be recovering in wolf territory.

Foxes, hawks, owls, badgers, and pine martens also benefit: more prey is available to them with fewer coyotes competing for the same food.

Grizzly bears chase wolves from their kills, helping themselves to quality food.

GRIZZLY BEARS ARE MUCH BIGGER than wolves and can chase them away from their kills, so wolf kills provide food for grizzlies, especially in the spring and fall. In addition, the wolves don't usually eat every last scrap of meat from their kills, so the number of scavengers, like ravens and eagles, has increased in the park.

Wolves on the hunt keep the elk on the move, spreading out their feeding.

WITHOUT WOLVES, the elk would linger along the streams in the park, sheltered from the wind, eating the shoots of willows and aspens before they had a chance to grow. Now the elk must keep on the move to make it harder for the wolves to find them. They tend to spend more time in open, grassy country where they can see danger coming, or along the edges of the forest, where they can escape more easily.

Young aspens, cottonwoods, and willows can grow again, and the animals that need them are also coming back.

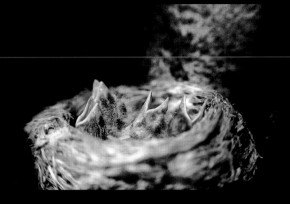

WITH THE ELK on the move, willows in particular are making a comeback. As the plants they depend upon recover, the beavers are also returning. In 1996 only one beaver colony lived in the far northern part of the park. By 2003 there were nine.

Scientists hope birds that hunt from aspens, like great gray owls, and songbirds that nest along the shores of ponds, such as the dusky flycatcher, will also become more common.

Returning the wolf is helping to make Yellowstone whole again.

A NATURAL SYSTEM LIKE Yellowstone is very complex. The weather is different every year. If summer brings enough rain and sun for the plants to prosper and if the winter is mild, the elk will prosper. The next year, the wolves will feast and trim the elk population, and so on. Thus, the balance of nature is always changing. But when all the pieces of the puzzle are present, the extremes are eliminated. Scientists hope that as the years go by, even more plants and animals that have become rare in the park will return. Today, Yellowstone is working its way back to a changing but healthy system, thanks to the wolves' return.

A NOTE ABOUT THE PHOTOGRAPHS

The wildlife photographs in this book were taken of wild animals in the Yellowstone ecosystem and have not been digitally altered. They were all taken by Dan Hartman and Cassie Hartman, with the exception of the following:

Pages 4–5: (Visitors pose on Mammoth Terrace) Unknown photographer, National Park Service (NPS). Page 5: (Giant geyser) Detroit Photographic Co., 1902, NPS. Page 7: (Car parked by Old Faithful Geyser) Unknown photographer, NPS; (Early tourist feeding a black bear) Unknown photographer, NPS; (Hunters on Yellowstone Lake) F. J. Haines, 1883, NPS. Page 9: (Visitors feeding deer) Unknown photographer, 1924, NPS. Pages 20–21: (Firefighter in burn near Lava Creek) Jeff Henry, 1988, NPS. Page 21: (Bull elk passing through a burned forest) Unknown photographer, 1988, NPS; (Burned trees near Black-tailed Plateau) Jim Peaco, 1988, NPS.

FOR MORE INFORMATION

Bearman's Yellowstone Outdoor Adventures!
www.yellowstone-bearman.com/wolves.html

Berger, Melvin and Gilda. *Howl! A Book About Wolves*. New York: Scholastic, 2002.

Howker, Janni. *Walk with a Wolf*. Cambridge, MA: Candlewick Press, 2002.

Markle, Sandra. *Growing Up Wild: Wolves*. New York: Atheneum, 2001.

Patent, Dorothy Hinshaw. *Gray Wolf, Red Wolf*. New York: Clarion Books, 1994.

Patent, Dorothy Hinshaw. *Yellowstone Fires: Flames and Rebirth*. New York: Holiday House, 1990.

Petersen, David. *Yellowstone National Park*. CT: Children's Press, 2001.

Swinburne, Stephen R. *Once a Wolf: How Wildlife Biologists Fought to Bring Back the Gray Wolf*. Boston, MA: Houghton Mifflin, 1999.

Vogel, Carole Garbuny. *The Great Yellowstone Fire*. Boston, MA: Little Brown, 1993.

Yellowstone National Park
www.yellowstonenationalpark.com/wolves.htm

Yellowstone's Wildlife: Wolf
www.yellowstone.net/wildlife/wolf.htm

Yellowstone Wolves
www.yellowstonewolves.org

INDEX

Elk

Aspens

Songbirds

Beavers

Moose

Wolves

Eagles

Bears